CUPID

His wing is the fan of a lady,
his foot's an invisible thing;
And his arrow is tipped with a jewel,
and shot from a silver string.

Victorian Keepsake

When first I saw thee dearest one,
Chief among the young and fair,
Little did I think that then,
Cupid's self was lurking there
Knew not till I felt the dart,
Thou hadst borne away my heart!

Allison Kyle Leopold's

Victorian Keepsake

Select Expressions of
Affectionate Regard
from the Romantic
Nineteenth Century

DOUBLEDAY
NEW YORK LONDON TORONTO SYDNEY AUCKLAND

SPECIAL CREDITS

Special Consultant: Joanne L. Cassullo
Photography: Edward Addeo

PUBLISHED BY DOUBLEDAY

a division of Bantam Doubleday Dell Publishing Group, Inc.
666 Fifth Avenue, New York, New York 10103

DOUBLEDAY and the portrayal of an anchor with a dolphin
are registered trademarks of Doubleday,
a division of Bantam Doubleday Dell Publishing Group, Inc.

Book Design by Viola Adams

Library of Congress Cataloging-in-Publication Data
Leopold, Allison Kyle.
[Victorian keepsake]
Allison Kyle Leopold's Victorian keepsake : select expressions of affectionate regard from
the romantic nineteenth century.—1st ed.
p.   cm.
1. Valentines—History—19th century.   2. Great Britain—Social life and customs.   3. United
States—Social life and customs.   I. Title.   II. Title: Victorian keepsake.
GT4925.L46   1991
394.2′683—dc20   90-19330
                                                                                            CIP

ISBN 0-385-41367-X

1   3   5   7   9   10   8   6   4   2

November 1991
First Edition

*To my family
for their
Love*

Good wishes for you

Table of Contents

A loveless marriage is an unchaste union.

—EVE'S DAUGHTERS, OR COMMON SENSE FOR MAID, WIFE, AND MOTHER, 1882

Introduction

$\mathcal{T}$he rituals and rules that the Victorians applied to almost every aspect of daily life—from the clothing that they wore to the furnishings with which they lived, to their manner of walking, talking, traveling, eating, greeting, and more—pertained, very definitely, to their world of romantic love. From the 1830s through the first decade of the twentieth century these rules, these codes and canons of acceptable etiquette, were a powerful force in shaping the pattern of daily life and behavior. And, as chaste and proper as that behavior may appear to us today, the romantic legacy left behind was a lasting one. In truth, the nineteenth century reveled in the glories of romantic love, celebrating it tenderly, affectionately, sentimentally, and yes, passionately, with a fervor and a flavor all its own.

One of the strongest clues we have to the deeply romantic Victorian nature is their evocative (and today, charmingly picturesque) vocabulary of love. Scores of sentimental songs, stories, and nineteenth-century novels abound with "blushing sweethearts," with "suitors," "swains," and "ardent beaux." Gentlemen and ladies "courted"; then "kept company." Affections were "wooed" and won; the prettiest girls were "spoken for." Intentions were "declared," hands and hearts pledged in "undying affection," and, at some point, most certainly, "liberties" were taken.

The Victorians left behind other evidence of the character of their amorous entanglements . . . their delicately yellowing love letters—florid "heartfelt" phrases elucidating "fondest hopes" in impossibly embellished and fading script; their earnest discourses on coquetry and flirtation: twirl a fan in your right hand and you callously announced, "I love another." Hold its ivory handle to your lips: "Kiss me." A declaration of feeling between a lady and a gentleman could be discreetly conveyed, without uttering a word, in an elegant floral duet.

He offers a red rose, symbolizing "I love you." She admits at least partial reciprocation with a purple pansy—"You occupy my thoughts." He presses further, sending everlasting pea—"Wilt thou go with me?" She replies with a daisy: "I will think of it." He, emboldened, presents a bloom known as shepherd's purse: "I offer you my all." She, doubting, retreats with a sprig of laurel: "Words, though sweet, may deceive." He persists—heliotrope: "I adore you." She, relenting, with zinnias—"I mourn your absence."

Perhaps most tellingly, though, the Victorians left us their valentines—lavish, layered confections of intertwined hearts and silken ribbons, filigreed with gilded, perforated paper lace and rich with quilted satin and velvet inserts. Many were so elaborate, so extravagant with embellishment (and often complex, folding construction), that they were even sent in protective boxes. It was through these often hand-decorated labors of love that people spoke their hearts, in achingly sentimental verse.

Take this token of affection.
May its beauty move thy heart.
Chill me not with cold rejection,
Bid not all my hopes depart!

or

Tho far away from thee I roam,
Forget thee I can never;
For all the joy this life affords
Is centered in thee ever.

May the flowers I send, breathe of my love.

3

Looking at Victorian valentines, there can be no question that these missals of innocent, decorative excess were also ones of profound passion. The flowery, loving, now hopelessly clichéed messages they contained were accepted literally—by the giver and the recipient—tributes to the touching emotional haze through which Victorian men and women alike viewed their world.

How *did* Victorian people meet, mate, wed, and bed? In their highly structured society, how did they manage to stumble from tentative introduction to genteel friendship, to blushing courtship, to final wedded intimacies? For many, the path to the nuptial altar was fraught with perils: for gentlemen at a dance, remembering *never* to encircle the waist of a lady until the music commenced— and immediately dropping one's arm when it ceased. For ladies, there was the risk of a courtship conducted at what were called "unseasonable" hours. Proper parlor chats and entertainments (under the scrutiny of a chaperone), walks, the occasional carriage

ride, all provided ample opportunity for the study of mutual tastes and feelings, everyone knew. A protracted visit by a gentleman till a too late hour, however, could easily incite gossip, the loss of one's reputation, and, if one wasn't careful, compromise, scandal, and ruin. No question, unless one conformed to the rules, Victorian courtship could be one bumpy buggy ride.

The answers, though, were all there—in the etiquette books, in the advice columns of the magazines (a major influence, by the way, in those pre-television, pre-radio days), and in dozens of other social aids. For tongue-tied and timid gentlemen, there were "valentine writers"—pocket-size handbooks to assist in the composition of verses guaranteed to win the purest feminine heart. During the 1850s, one such booklet, "The People's Valentine Writer," offered acrostics for one's beloved Charlotte, Eliza, Jane, or Fanny. This somewhat rocky rhyme, not to mention sentiment, was penned for a Victorian Laura.

L ess of friendship, more of love,

A single smile, my heart can move;

U ndying love! not echoed yet,

R emains within a pond'rous weight

A nd, without you, I'm all but dead.

During the 1870s and 1880s *Hill's Manual* was but one of the guides which steered earnest couples through love's mazes, notable for its carefully worded suggestions as to favorable and unfavorable replies to letters, letters that declared love at first sight (apparently a more frequent occurrence than one would imagine), as well as letters that graciously accepted or declined proposals of marriage. It should be noted that, in some circles, well-bred young ladies were advised to decline once or even twice—for modesty's sake— the suitors they secretly hoped to accept.

Courting rituals like these, as well as other carefully prescribed conduct, made it easier for a society that was new and uncertain to define itself. And the rituals represented the norm. Gentlemen incurred no embarrassment by indulging in the era's often over-wrought sentimentality of expression. Rather, it was simply the way things were done. "Dear, dear Clara, you cannot be indifferent to the fact that I have long devotedly loved you; and at the hour of parting, I feel that I cannot go without telling you my heart, and asking you if I may not have your love in return?" During the 1880s, this was phrasing sanctioned by *Hill's Manual* for a young man proposing marriage and the bold but uncertain adventure of emigration to the West. The gushing sentimentalism that makes us smile today was partly a consequence of the innocence of a far more tender, far less sophisticated time than our own—a time accustomed to, and comfortable with, the literal sincerity of effusive, rapturous emotion. Also it was, in some way, an escape from the uncertainty and confusion of a world that was rapidly undergoing change, the accelerated pace of industrialism looming, a new, faster, harsher century beckoning. Romantic ritual, sentiment, and unrelenting decorative prettiness softened and sweetened life's edges, promising to keep things, at least for a time, sheltered, secure, and genteel.

Tangible evidence of the Victorians' sentimental absorption can be found in the everyday artifacts of their domestic life: the decorative patterns on their dishes, carpets, wallpapers, and uphol-

stery; the subject matter of the prints and paintings that hung on their walls; the unrelenting prettiness of the illustrations that filled their journals and magazines. This was a world that tended to sentimentalize the most mundane things—from a design embossed on a teacup to a toothbrush. Small wonder that they sentimentalized the already sentimental world of love itself!

A large portion of the era's purely romantic artifacts—dance programs and chromolithographed calling cards decorated with doves and flowers, love letters and fans, lockets engraved with cherubs—have been saved and passed down to us today. People cherished these tokens of love, tucking them away in round, paper-covered bandboxes or at the bottom of leather-bound trunks. In all of these items the Victorian passion for elaborate ornament is evident. Marriage licenses weren't the staid official certificates we know today but, rather, charming, surprisingly lively documents, often adorned with images of brightly colored, trilling birds, cooing doves, floating ribbons, and dimpled cupids. Calling cards shyly proclaim, "Think of me when far away." Even a fragile silken bookmark whispers, "Unchanging Love."

It is these items and others that bring to life the dicta of the etiquette books, that show us as well as tell us how the game of love was once played: with letters of introduction and formal permissions to court . . . with calling cards and posies . . . with invitations to balls, dances, skating fetes and sociables, picnics and private theatricals. And intentions had to be declared. Neither party had the right to dally with the other's affections if those intentions weren't "honorable," i.e., marriage. Love was, people knew, a serious matter. "If rightly mated in the conjugal state, life will be one continual joy," they were instructed. "If unhappily wedded, the soul will be forever yearning, and never satisfied; happiness may be hoped for, may be dreamed of, may be the object ever labored for, but it will never be realized."

Some of the sentiments and traditions assembled here still have the ring of truth about them; even today they make inherent sense.

Insights regarding the natures of men and women hold fast. "Never reproach the other for an error which was done with a good motive and with the best judgement at the time," would-be husbands and wives were wisely counseled. "Let the rebuke be preceded by a kiss." Other maxims, though, despite the passage of the same amount of time, have become merely quaint, notions peculiar to our sweeter, gentler past: "A very grave responsibility has the man assumed in his marriage. Doting parents have confided to his care the welfare of a loved daughter and a trusting woman has risked all her future happiness in his keeping. Largely it will depend upon him whether her pathway shall be strewn with thorns or roses."

The intention here is more than just the provocation of nostalgic wonder at the bygone customs of a bygone age. Instead, it is hoped that these traditions will be seen as a window into Victorian times, illuminating the values and aspirations of the people who followed them. Viewed this way, they can be taken not merely as mores of an era obsessed with sentiment but as expressions of a rich and complex society. —Allison Kyle Leopold

A bow or graceful inclination should be made by ladies when rec-ognizing their acquaintances of the opposite sex. It is the privilege of the lady to bow first. —1884

PREMATURE DECLARATION

It is very injudicious, not to say presumptuous, for a gentleman to make a proposal to a young lady on too brief an acquaintance. A lady who would accept a gentleman at first sight can hardly possess the discretion needed to make a good wife.   —1879

Promise you'll be mine for life, say you'll be my little wife.
Love and kisses we will share, never knowing any care.

Courtship, Manners & Morals

*Being the rules of etiquette and deportment
for decorous and acceptable flirtation and
coquetry for those hoping to advance
from genteel acquaintanceship
to blessed intimacy*

Ah, the wily dance of Victorian courtship! There's a sense of expectancy and nostalgia that lingers in the very sound of the phrase. It signaled the commencement of dozens of now charmingly old-fashioned rituals that tenderly careened its willing participants between persuasion and propriety, ever dangling the promise of mutual joy.

At about age sixteen or perhaps eighteen, young women began to plan for this rite of passage, eagerly anticipating invitations to balls and entertainments, calls from hopeful suitors, a whirl of gaiety and delight. The convention of paying calls allowed young women of marriageable age to meet eligible men; flirting—that mainstay of courtship—was the socially acceptable way for ladies to respond to suitors who interested them, gently rebuff ones who didn't, as well as discreetly broadcast their attraction to those whose attentions they would welcome. Though not difficult, courtship did have its intricacies, gentle artifices for both sexes to master: how to accept, defer, decline, encourage within the confines of social conventions that insisted on a rigorous formality. Couples, for example, addressed each other as "Miss" or "Mister" unless they had known each other from childhood; men were cautioned not to seat themselves next to their hostesses on the parlor sofa unless specifically invited to do so.

Behind the frivolity and gambit, though—a gentleman's exaggerated gallantries and deference, the flounced dance dresses a young lady was now permitted to wear, the endless exchange of bows and curtsies, protests and proclamations, love notes, bouquets, and trinkets—there was, of course, serious purpose: the search for, the wooing and winning of one's heart's beloved.

Choose as the partner of your heart, your home, your life, a good sound, clean-hearted man who loves you and wins your love by the development of tastes congenial with yours; a man whom, as a friend, you could esteem and admire were he the husband of another. That is a test that would shake a mere fancy into thin air.

—*OUR DEPORTMENT, OR THE MANNERS, CONDUCT AND DRESS OF THE MOST REFINED SOCIETY*, 1882

From A Gentleman's Conduct Toward Ladies

As soon . . . as, a man neglects all others, to devote himself to a single lady, he gives that lady reason to suppose that he is particularly attracted to her, and may give her cause to believe that she is to become engaged to him, without telling her so. A gentleman who does not contemplate matrimony should not pay too exclusive attention to any one lady.

From A Lady's Conduct Toward Gentlemen

A young lady should not encourage the addresses of a gentleman unless she feels that she can return his affections. It is the prerogative of a man to propose and of a woman to accept or refuse, and a lady of tact and kind heart will exercise her prerogative before her suitor is brought to the humiliation of an offer which must result in refusal.
—OUR DEPORTMENT, OR THE MANNERS, CONDUCT AND DRESS OF THE MOST REFINED SOCIETY, 1882

A gentleman is always distinguished by his respectful attention to women.
—GOOD MORALS AND GENTLE MANNERS, 1873

Fairy, to her my passion move.   *Whisper 'neath her ringlets that I love,*

Fairy on her moulded bosom press,   *Thy rosy fingers to yield a happiness.*

Do not force Love's fruitage into insipid maturity. Still less suffer every chance comer to handle the ripening peach to see if it will suit his royal fancy until the down is all gone before the rightful claimant appears.

—EVE'S DAUGHTERS, OR COMMON SENSE FOR MAID, WIFE, AND MOTHER. 1882

The stars may fall, the sun decay,
The earth's whole fabric waver,
But firm as heaven my love shall stay,
Unquenched, unceasing never.

Familiarity.—No girl should permit a boy to be so familiar as to toy with her hands, or play with her rings; to handle her curls or encircle her waist with his arm. Such impudent intimacy should never be tolerated for a moment. No gentleman will attempt it; no lady will permit it.

—*GOOD MORALS AND GENTLE MANNERS,* 1873.

THE ONLY TWO AT THE OPERA

Do not make the public room the arena for torturing any simple swain who perchance may admire you a little more than you deserve. Having ourselves passed the age of soft hopes and feverish anxieties therefrom resulting, we have often been calm spectators of such a scene as the above: recollect that while you are wounding another's heart, you may be trifling with your own peace.

—*TRUE POLITENESS, THE LADIES BOOK OF ETIQUETTE,* C. 1870s

CONVERSING WITH LADIES

A gentleman should never lower the intellectual standard of his conversation in addressing ladies. Pay them the compliment of seeming to consider them capable of an equal understanding with gentlemen. You will, no doubt, be somewhat surprised to find in how many cases the supposition will be grounded on fact, and in the few instances where it is not, the ladies will be pleased rather than offended at the delicate compliment you pay them. When you "come down" to commonplace or small-talk with an intelligent lady, one of two things is the consequence; she either recognizes the condescension and despises you, or else she accepts it as the highest intellectual effort of which you are capable and rates you accordingly.

On Hearing an Indelicate Word or Expression which Allows No Possible Harmless Interpretation

Then not a shadow of a smile should flit across the lips. Either complete silence should be preserved in return, or the words, "I do not understand you," be spoken. A lady will always fail to hear that which she should not hear, or having unmistakably heard, she will not understand. —OUR DEPORTMENT, 1882

Printed & Published by J. WRIGLEY, 25, Miller-st., Manchester.

Tho' small the pledge yet may it be,
Remembrance of my love to thee,
And may thy love delight my breast,
Possessing all of thee possest.

Printed & Published by J. WRIGLEY, 25, Miller-st., Manchester

I'd have, my love, a happy home, (just what a home should be,)
A home of peace, a home of love, as made by thee and me,
When true affection warms the breast, and dreams like these depart,
It matters little what's our lot, love's home is in the heart.

Tokens of Love & Romantic Enticements

Being the cards, love notes, floral tributes, and other affectionate tokens of sincere regard, as well as fans, fragrances, and elements of enticement permissible in the arena of genteel seduction

*O*rnamented calling cards, carefully composed love notes, valentines bearing hidden messages of love, dewy bouquets of flowers, and gilded volumes of misty-eyed poetry were among the tokens of love which the Victorians employed in order to flirt, tempt, seduce, and cajole their would-be lovers.

They were sheltered, of course, by the taut boundaries of their manners. "Especially never offer a lady a gift of great cost," preached *Decorum, A Practical Treatise on Etiquette and Dress,* written in 1879. "It is in the highest degree indelicate. . . ." Most other advice manuals concurred. Confectionery and flowers were universally deemed "safe"; being of a perishable, ephemeral nature, no great significance could be attached to their receipt. Sheet music, poetry books or albums, and items like card cases were also respectable offerings, although there were those paragons whose scruples frowned on their propriety, counseling young women to accept flowers and nothing else.

21

When the golden sun is
sinking
And your heart from care
is free

When o 'er thousand things
you 're thinking
Will you sometimes
think of me?

Ladies, of course, refrained from offering gentlemen any such love tokens, unless they had received ones first. This was a sensible precaution, it was felt, to prevent feminine "compromise." At a certain point (perhaps with talk of an engagement in the offing) a lady might be so bold as to bestow some handmade (and therefore even more precious) trifle on an especially favored suitor. Whether a pretty pencil sketch, a bit of decoratively worked needlework or, even better, an artistically arranged scrap album, he of course was expected to greet such tokens with nothing less than ecstatic rapture.

Ladies were permitted to engage in other sorts of time-honored enticements to hurry the course of romantic love. They coquettishly fluttered fans of painted ivory or feathers, set off their milky complexions with filmy lace collars and pearl-encrusted brooches, and, at the grandest of soirees, adorned themselves with glittering gems. Homemade balms brightened feminine eyes and reddened pale lips, while the faint odor of lavender, violets, or essence of roses, clinging to the hair or shoulders, could be alluring indeed.

All of this was considered fair and even proper. "If a gentleman asks a lady to accompany him to the opera or a concert, she has no right to turn that expected pleasure into a pain and mortification by presenting herself with tumbled hair, ill-chosen dress, badly fitting gloves and an atmosphere of cheap and offensive perfumes," according to the authors of Decorum. "Duty has more to do with attention to the toilette than vanity." In addition, a woman who was careless of her appearance actually risked being regarded as equally careless concerning the purity of her character, while the lady who indulged in the finest of silk gloves, who tastefully displayed sparkling trinkets and tucked fragrant blooms in her hair was exhibiting evidence of refinement, a highly desirable trait in a wife-to-be. These acts marked her as "possessed of those instincts of grace, which, rightly directed, will beautify and embellish all her surroundings through life."

ON LETTERS OF LOVE

The Victorians expressed their thoughts in far more letters than we do today—from letters of introduction to letters of friendship, letters to schoolmates who had married or moved away, letters requesting the loan of opera glasses or money, letters advising young men against the dangers of "bad company" and more. Of these letters that were composed, it was acknowledged that the love letter should be the most carefully prepared missive of all. Grammar and wording should be thoroughly checked lest an error interfere with the writer's prospects, making him or her sport for ridicule. Correspondence, in most cases, should be undertaken only with the approval of the lovers' parents. Most of all, it was advised, love letters should be thoroughly read and reread before sending as they not only were most surely to be cherished and preserved, but also most likely to be regretted in later life.

As a rule, young ladies were warned to maintain their dignity when writing letters of love, lest, if their feelings changed, they should despair of ever having written the letter at all. Young men were inclined to be more effusive, bolder, poetic, and yes, sentimental. And, for both sexes, *Hill's Manual* and other popular etiquette guides supplied scores of perfectly proper examples on which they could model their own.

Elaborate calling cards of all kinds were exchanged by Victorian friends and lovers, who adored their brilliant colorings, rich designs, the opportunity to offer a tender endearment—"With fondest greetings"—as well as the novelty of their smooth, sensuous surfaces. These were oh, so discreet "hidden name" cards, usually sent by gentlemen, which featured a bit of ornamental scrap (usually a bouquet of flowers) shielding the admirer's name, as well as miniature, hand-painted calling cards, delicately worded "acquaintance" cards, and other sentimental tokens.

BLINDNESS

"Is she tall or short?" I never thought.
"Is she dark or fair?" You got me there.
Be she fair as day or black as night,
All I've observed is, she's just right.
"Is she six feet high or four foot three?"
Her height's the height that just suits me.—

HARPER'S BAZAR, FEBRUARY 20, 1897

"You are the only woman I have ever loved, darling," he
whispered after she had accepted him. "Impossible," said she.
"I know better. You make love like an old hand; you cannot
deceive me, George."

—HARPER'S BAZAR, FEBRUARY 16, 1895

AT WHAT AGE
TO WRITE LOVE LETTERS

The love letter is the prelude to marriage—a state that, if the husband and wife be fitted for each other, is the most natural and serenely happy; a state, however, that none should enter upon, until in judgment and physical development, both parties have completely matured. Many a life has been wrecked by a blind, impulsive marriage, simply resulting from a youthful passion. As a physiological law, man should be twenty-five, and woman twenty-three, before marrying. —HILL'S MANUAL, 1884

Go little
valentine
to Earl.
So many
miles away.
And carry
to him
all my
This v.

The love letter should be honest. It should say what the writer means and no more. For the lady or gentleman to play the part of a coquette, studying to see how many lovers he or she may secure is very disreputable and bears in its train a long list of sorrows, frequently wrecking domestic happiness for a lifetime. —*HILL'S MANUAL.* 1884

A love letter should be dignified in tone and expressive of esteem
and affection. It should be free from silly and extravagant expressions and contain nothing of which the writer would be ashamed
were the letter to fall under the eyes of any person beside the one to
whom it was written.

—*POLITE LIFE AND ETIQUETTE, OR WHAT IS RIGHT AND THE SOCIAL ARTS,* 1891

THE ART & PROPRIETY OF GIFT GIVING . . .

The gifts made by ladies to gentlemen are of the most refined nature possible: they should be little articles not purchased, but deriving a priceless value as being the offspring of their gentle skill; a little picture from their pencil, or a trifle from their needle. —DECORUM, 1879

Aside from the engagement-ring, a gentleman should not, at this period of acquaintance, make expensive presents to his intended bride. Articles of small value, indicative of respect and esteem, are all that should pass between them. Should the marriage take place, and coming years of labor crown their efforts with success, then valuable gifts will be much more appropriate than in the earlier years of their acquaintance. —HILL'S MANUAL, 1884

Jewelry will always be in vogue for valentine presents. Rings, pendants and pins are the most usual of selection; jewelers also show an endless variety of purses, bonbonnieres and vinaigrettes in shining silver. Pincushions come also in many shapes; a novelty in these is made from two large, silver hearts joining as a receptacle for bonnet pins. —THE LADIES' HOME JOURNAL, FEBRUARY 1893

A tribute
of affection.

Let light shine thro' this card and see
The plaque of curiosity!
May you, with care, have more success

A word or more is not out of place concerning the kind of gifts that a young man may make with propriety to a young woman with whom he is on agreeable terms. Flowers, books, candy,—these are gifts that he may make without offense, and she may receive without undue or unpleasant sense of obligation. . . . If a young man is engaged to a young woman, the possible choice of gifts is much enlarged. Even then, however, very expensive gifts are not desirable. They lessen somewhat the charm of the relation between the two.

—*EVERYDAY ETIQUETTE, A PRACTICAL MANUAL OF SOCIAL USAGES,* 1907

33

Some Other Ideas . . .

*Books and pictures are favorite valentine selections and may be
purchased at any and all prices. Of course, volumes of poetry and
love stories lend themselves much more readily as appropriate to
the season than essays or histories, but any favorite book cannot
fail to please. Photographs, etchings, engravings, and water colors
are framed daintily in white and gold or white and silver and
make charming offerings . . . Frames of silver for card photographs are heart-shaped and come singly or in pairs. Many are
engraved with mottos.*

*Writing tablets, portfolios for stationery, glove boxes, photograph
cases are all welcome gifts to any girl sweetheart as they may be
kept in daily use as reminders of the absent fiancé. Sachets for
handkerchiefs, veils, laces and gloves are extensively used.*

—THE LADIES' HOME JOURNAL, FEBRUARY 1893

May true
friends
be around
you

FLOWERS AND SWEETS

Flowers, besides being an eminently acceptable gift of courtship, played an important part in the wooing and winning of one's lady love. One had to be careful, though, what kind of flowers one sent. The "language of flowers" (and most etiquette books offered translations), an elaborate floral code, assigned different meanings to different blooms, thus allowing many a shy young swain to send a bouquet which delicately suggested what he dared not say aloud.

Loving
Greeting

Flowers make, of course, the most usual offering, the only objection which can be found against them being their perishability. Loose clusters of single kinds of blossoms, roses, lilies of the valley, daffodils or white lilacs will be much used. Set pieces in the form of horseshoes, hearts or baskets of fancy shapes are filled with smaller blossoms and tied with satin ribbons of harmonizing colors. With these, and indeed with any valentine gift, must be sent not only the donor's card but a love message inscribed thereon which will do quite as much as the beautiful gift itself to gladden the eyes and heart of the happy Valentine. —THE LADIES' HOME JOURNAL, FEBRUARY 1893

ACCEPT this message,
    Dearest, I pray,
  From one who loves you,
    'Tis Valentine's Day.

A profusion of flowers in the hands of the women (at a ball) should add their brightness and perfume to the rooms. The great number of bouquets sent to a debutante is often embarrassing. The present fashion is to have them hung, by different ribbons, on the arm, so that they look as if almost trimming a dress. —POLITE LIFE AND ETIQUETTE, 1891

1891
Bachelor's Button . . . Hope in Love
Yellow Carnation . . . Disdain
Rose-colored Chrysanthemum . . .
In Love Columbine . . . Folly

Bon-bons will also be sent in fancy boxes and baskets and dainty booklets ornamented with ribbons, laces and flowers. The hackneyed "sweets to the sweet" is but one of the many quotations found attached to these pretty favorites. A few others are: "Love has found the way." "My love is deep, the more I give to thee." "A wilderness of sweets." "Love, thou art every day my Valentine."
—THE LADIES' HOME JOURNAL, FEBRUARY 1893

DRESS, JEWELS, AND
OTHER ADORNMENT . . .

The desire of exhibiting an amiable exterior is essentially requisite in a young lady, for it indicates cleanliness, sweetness, a love of order and propriety and all of those virtues which are attractive to their associates, and particularly those of the other sex. —DECORUM. 1879

Perfumes are a necessary appendage to the toilet; let them be delicate, not powerful; the attar of roses is the most elegant; the Heduesmia is at once fragrant and delicate. Many others may be named, equally refined; but recollect that none must be patronized which are so obtrusive as to give the idea that they are not indulged in as a luxury but used from necessity.

—TRUE POLITENESS, 1878

Perfumes, if used at all, should be used in the strictest moderation, and be of the most recherché kind. Musk and patchouli should always be avoided, as to many people of sensitive temperament, their odor is exceedingly disagreeable. Cologne water of the best quality is never offensive. —OUR DEPORTMENT, 1882

ON THE FLUTTER OF FANS . . .
IN PARLORS AND AT PARTIES,
A SIGN OF GENTILITY AND GRACE

A Request

"Just why you need a fan, Marie,
Is what, try as I may, I cannot see,"
said he.
"You're always so cold—to me!
In fact, so cold are you
It makes me fairly blue!
So put aside the fan, lay it apart,
and let old shimmering sol melt down your icy heart."

—HARPER'S BAZAR, OCTOBER 5, 1895

DRESS FOR THE OPERA

The fan, the bouquet and handkerchief must all have due consideration and be in keeping with the other proportions of the dress.

—DECORUM, 1879

Fans make very beautiful and useful gifts for valentine purposes. Last year they were used for this purpose more extensively than any other feminine article. They are made of gauze, silk, satin or feathers and are decorated with hand painting, embroidery, laces and spangles, the sticks and handles being of ivory, sandalwood, silver or ebony. . . . Sachets for holding fans are also to be found.

—THE LADIES' HOME JOURNAL, FEBRUARY 1893

At a Ball

A single string of pearls or a gemmed heart hung around her neck offer no real defiance to the fixed canon that a fresh-faced young woman does not need jewels.

—ENCYCLOPAEDIA OF ETIQUETTE, A BOOK OF MANNERS FOR EVERYDAY USE, 1901

Never wear mosaic gold or paste diamonds; they are representative of a mean ambition to appear what you are not, and most likely what you ought not to wish to be.   —TRUE POLITENESS, C. 1878

Jewelry is out of place in any of the errands which take a lady from her home in the morning.   —DECORUM, 1879

On the Wearing of Gloves . . .

That "a lady is known by her gloves and her boots" has passed into a proverb, so any carelessness or untidiness in these important details will place her "beyond the pale." —CORRECT SOCIAL USAGE, 1907

Gloves are worn by gentlemen as well as ladies in the street, at an evening party, at the opera or theatre, at receptions, at church, when paying a call, riding or driving, but not in the country or at dinner. White should be worn at balls; the palest colors at evening parties and neutral colors at church. . . . —OUR DEPORTMENT, 1882

. . . Never be seen without gloves in a ball-room; or with those of any color other than white, unless they are the most delicate hue. —OUR DEPORTMENT, 1882

No gentleman should use his bare hand to press the waist of a lady in the waltz. If without gloves, carry a handkerchief in the hand. —HILL'S MANUAL, 1884

Gloves must always harmonize with your dress; and it need scarcely be observed that they must always be clean. Nothing can be more vulgar than high, glaring coloured gloves: the primrose (and the white for evening parties) are decidedly the most elegant, if your dress will admit of their being worn. —TRUE POLITENESS, C. 1878

Deep and bright colored gloves are always in bad taste; very few persons are careful enough in selecting gloves. —DECORUM, 1879

When a lady has taken her seat at the dinner table, she should at once remove her gloves; although occasionally long elbow gloves are not removed during dinner, but this is conspicuous and inconvenient. —MANNERS AND RULES OF GOOD SOCIETY, 1913

On Beauty . . .

Young women who neglect their toilet and manifest little concern about dress, indicate a general disregard of order—a mind but ill adapted to the details of housekeeping—a deficiency of taste and of the qualities that inspire love.

*Ah! Could you look into my heart
And watch your image there!
You would own the sunny loveliness
Affection makes it wear.*

—HILL'S MANUAL, 1884

*It is every woman's duty to make herself as beautiful as possible;
and no less the duty of every man to make himself pleasing in
appearance.* —DECORUM, 1879

*This love of personal adornment being an inherent, desirable, refin-
ing element of character, it does not, therefore, become us to ignore
or to suppress it. On the contrary, it should be our duty to cultivate
neatness of appearance and artistic arrangement in dress, the whole
being accompanied by as much personal beauty as possible.*

—HILL'S MANUAL, 1884

How to be beautiful, and consequently powerful, is a question of far greater importance to the feminine mind than predestination or any other abstract subject. If women are to govern, control, manage, influence, and retain the adoration of husbands, fathers, brothers, lovers, or even cousins, they must look their prettiest at all times. —POLITE LIFE AND ETIQUETTE, 1891

Love's Proper Pastimes

*Being a guide to proper parlor pastimes, dances,
picnics, parties, games & gaieties, sporting events
and other discreet activities in which the
courting set may indulge*

The parlor was the main stage on which the drama of Victorian courtship was played. There, ladies received their gentleman callers; there gentlemen, holding their hats gracefully on their laps, attempted such bright and witty conversation as was considered proper and exchanged confidences over tea. Each would be sufficiently well mannered to avoid politics or religious matters, or "any subject of absorbing nature likely to lead to discussion." In the large drawing rooms they enjoyed the frolic of private theatricals, concerts, parlor pastimes such as "tableaux vivants" and yes— such wickedness!—even racy kissing games, like "To Kiss the Learned Pig."

Music could be of considerable benefit in the social life of a courting couple. Should both of them happen to play, the piano afforded the fortuitous opportunity for close physical contact: couples could sit cozily together, practicing duets or popular songs which—such luck!—called for the players' hands to cross. To be able to sing as well as play was a valued accomplishment for a young lady. Both these skills allowed her to "exhibit" at dinner parties and other home entertainments, and thereby come to the admiring notice of suitable men.

But courting took place in other places as well—at concerts, lecture halls and musicales, at fairs, sociables, and small parties known as "kettle-drums," and, most especially, out of doors. Victorian couples enjoyed picnics, garden parties, boating and nature walks, and rustic hiking parties in the woods. The appeal of the outdoors was apparent. At picnics, for example, ladies and gentlemen were "privileged" to relax many of the forms and ceremonies elsewhere required by etiquette. "Here men and women mingle for a day of pleasure in the woods or fields or on the water, and it is the part of all who attend to do what they can for their own and their neighbor's enjoyment." Horseback-riding—"one of the most exhilarating and enjoyable amusements that can be indulged in by either ladies or gentlemen"—and in the later part of the century activities such as golf, tennis, croquet, and other sports were enjoyed. Interest in roller skating and ice skating soared, probably because such sports enabled willing couples to hold hands. Archery allowed not only a measure of physical contact— gentlemen instructing ladies in proper form—but, for ladies, figure-revealing postures as well. "As a graceful, healthful and innocent sport, it has no equal among any of the games that have been introduced where both sexes participate," demurred the author of one popular etiquette guide. As for the bicycle craze of the 1890s, it certainly offered advantages other than mere exercise: particularly, it permitted young people a measure of privacy as they were able to ride off together, away from watchful eyes, all under the guise of healthful activity.

Most popular of all, throughout the Victorian years, were the balls and dances—the lively music, the fancy dress, the stirring, festive atmosphere enhanced by the heavy scent of an abundance of flowers, made these the most eagerly anticipated of events. Dancing promised an alluring closeness, a moment or two for a private whispered word. Ladies were warned, though, never to dance more than two dances with the same man, lest they incite unwholesome gossip. Yet another preservative of feminine virtue was the strictly observed dictum that ladies never enter or leave a ballroom unattended.

True gentlemen readily followed all the elaborate rituals: refraining from placing an ungloved hand on his lady's waist while waltzing; never presuming on the acquaintance of a lady after a ball (ballroom introductions closed with the dancing); and always, after dancing, conducting a lady to her seat. At that point he thanked her profusely for the joy and pleasure she had bestowed upon him, yet ever taking care not to tarry too long in intimate conversation. After the dance, he knew full well that she wasn't at all obliged to invite him to enter the house when he accompanied her home and, if so invited, he should decline the invitation. Requesting permission to call the next day or evening, though, was considered true politeness indeed.

Ladies should not boast to others, who dance but little, of the great number of dances for which they are engaged in advance.

—*HILL'S MANUAL*, 1884

BALLS AND DANCES

Recollect that your partner is for the time being your very humble servant, and that he will be honoured by acquiescing in any of your wishes: for instance, you may wish to promenade, to walk from one room to another, to join your friends; you may require a jelly, ice, wine, or any other refreshment; your dress may have become disarranged; in short he will feel honoured by receiving your commands, and he ought to anticipate your wishes on most of the above, and many more ordinary occasions. On no account be seen parading a ballroom by yourself.

If a gentleman presumes to ask you to dance without an introduction, you will of course, refuse. It is hardly necessary to supply the fair reader with words to repel such rudeness; but as some of the fair sex may by possibility be so surprised by it as not effectually to repel it at the moment, we will suggest that a man must have more than ordinary impertinence if he was not satisfied by your saying "I must decline, sir, not having the honour of your acquaintance;" and recollect that his previous rudeness ought to be punished by your refusing to be introduced. However mortifying to the individual this may be, rely upon it he will respect you the more for such decision.

—*TRUE POLITENESS, THE LADIES BOOK OF ETIQUETTE.* C. 1870s

Though not customary for a married couple to dance together in society, those men who wish to show their wives the compliment of such unusual attention, if they possess any independence, will not be deterred from doing so, by their fear of any comments from Mrs. Grundy. —*OUR DEPORTMENT.* 1882

You are Cordially Invited to be Present at the
Second Phantom Dance
of the season given in the
South Bethlehem Dancing Academy
Cor. Fourth and Wyandotte Sts.,
Friday Evening, March 21st, 1902.
Yours Respectfully,
Robt. F. Bauder, D. M.

CLASSES MONDAY AND THURSDAY EVENINGS. PARTIES AND MATINEES EVERY SATURDAY.

SONQUASSEN TRIBE, No. 2, I. O. R. M.
TRADING POST.
DANCING
Dec. 10th, 1891.
D. E. SANFORD, Floor Manager.

B. C. C.
Yourself and Ladies are cordially invited to attend a
Masquerade,
At Elmwood Creamery, on Wednesday Evening,
February 21st, 1883, at 8 P. M.
MUSIC BY BUSER.
Gentlemen will please present this ticket at the door
A. C. HOWELL,
W. P. TOLEMAN, } Committee.
J. K. ALEXANDER,

No condemnation is too great for that selfish and, sad to say, not uncommon man who, accepts a hostess' hospitality and requites it by standing in doorways, to feast his artistic appetite upon the agreeable sights and sounds of a beautiful ball-room, satisfies his hunger at her supper table, gossips a little with the men and few of the chaperons, and, after lingering an hour, takes his way home. There is but one greater offender in the social world—the man who can dance but is too lazy and self-indulgent to fulfil his mission and who haunts the smoking rooms while charming girls sit unappreciated beside their anxious chaperons.

—ENCYCLOPAEDIA OF ETIQUETTE, 1901.

"AFTER THE BALL: COMPARING PROGRAMMES"
FROM THE PICTURE BY ARTHUR HOPKINS

Only for large and ceremonious balls is it necessary to provide pro-gramme cards, though these printed lists are not only convenient they also serve as agreeable souvenirs of the occasion. . . . Pro-grammes are either placed in the dressing-rooms or piled on a tray in the hall where guests can help themselves.—At subscription and public balls young ladies should invariably be chaperoned. Each girl may bring her own matronly companion or by previous arrangement solicit and secure the chaperonage of some matron who is to be present whether as lady patroness or as the duenna for her own daughter. —CORRECT SOCIAL USAGE. 1907

Fancy dress balls are of frequent occurrence; but when the arrangements are carried out with spirit and ingenuity, they present a most unique, gay and imposing spectacle.

—MANNERS AND RULES OF GOOD SOCIETY.

1913

NO. 12 Masque Folder.

Encouraging

"Grace," he began, tenderly on New Year's Eve. "I—I—" when she interrupted him. "Wait until twelve o'clock," she whispered. "I had enough proposals last year to suit any one, but I want '94 to beat it—so please wait."

—HARPER'S BAZAR, JANUARY 6, 1894

···A GRAND···

LEAP YEAR PARTY

➤ BY ➤

EIGHT YOUNG LADIES

BIRD HALL, EAST WALPOLE.

* Thursday * Evening, * April * 12 * 1888. *

OTHER AMUSEMENTS . . .

There is great diversity in the forms of recreation which may be enjoyed by the young indoors. Some of these are ingenious, amusing and instructive. Every one in the company should join in any diversion which does not violate his conscience or sense of propriety. Any play that is rough and rude, in which there is danger of injury to persons, to furniture, or to clothing ought not to be tolerated in the house. . . . That amusement which permits any improper familiarity between the sexes is not in good taste. If the game requires the boys to catch and struggle, and wrestle with the girls, or even to put their hands upon their persons, or to kiss them, it is of very doubtful propriety. Such freedom is not consistent with that respect which the sexes should cultivate for each other.

—GOOD MORALS AND GENTLE MANNERS, 1873

*Private theatricals may be made very pleasing and instructive enter-
tainments for fall or winter evenings among either young or married
people. They include charades, proverbs, tableaux, dramatic readings
and the presentation of a short dramatical piece and be successfully
given in the parlor or drawing room. . . . Supper or refreshments usually follow private theatricals, of which both the performers and invited guests are invited to partake, and the remainder of the evening
is spent in social intercourse.*   —OUR DEPORTMENT, 1882

*Any lady guest being invited to play the piano, it is courtesy for the
gentleman nearest her to offer his arm and escort her to the instru-
ment. While she is playing, he will hold her bouquet, fan and gloves,
and should also turn the leaves if he can readily read music, but
he should not attempt it otherwise.*   —HILL'S MANUAL, 1884

It is the duty of the gentleman to be ever attentive to the ladies. If it be a picnic, the gentlemen will carry the luncheon, erect the swings, construct the tables, bring the water, provide the fuel for boiling the tea, etc. On the fishing excursion, they will furnish the tackle, bait the hooks, row the boats, carry the fish, and furnish comfortable seats for the ladies. In gathering nuts, they will climb the trees, do the shaking, carry the nuts and assist the ladies across streams and over fences. If possible, in crossing the fields, go through the bars or gateway, and avoid the necessity of compelling the ladies to clamber over the fences. Should it be necessary to climb them, it is etiquette for the gentleman to go over first, and when the lady is firmly on the top, he will gently help her down. —HILL'S MANUAL, 1884

Beverly, N. J., June 26, 1875.

Miss Bertha Hoffman

You are invited to

A Basket Picnic,

at Eddington Grove, on Thursday next, July 1st.

The company will meet on the beach, at the foot of Cooper street, at 8 o'clock.

Each lady will provide lunch for two.

HARRY BAUMGARDNER,
SAMUEL LOAG,
EDWARD J. THOMASON,
JOHN C. JENNINGS,
CLEMENT E. LLOYD,
Committee.

A girl should do well to remember that the man who has taken her boating is doing all the work and is trying to give her a pleasant time. She should meet him half-way, and should try to repress any nervousness she may experience in being on the water and any resentment she may feel at being occasionally requested by her "skipper" to "trim boat." —EVERYDAY ETIQUETTE. 1907

Of late years, ladies have taken very much to rowing; this can be easily managed in a quiet river or private pond, but it is scarcely to be attempted in the more crowded ad public parts of our rivers—at any rate, unless superintended by gentlemen. In moderation, it is capital exercise for ladies, but when they attempt it, they should bear in mind that they should assume a dress proper for the occasion. They should leave their crinolines at home, and wear a skirt barely touching the ground. . . . It is impossible for any lady to row with comfort or grace if she laces tightly. —DECORUM. 1879

An elegant skating costume may be of velvet, trimmed with fur, with fur bordered gloves and boots. Any of the warm, bright-colored wool fabrics, however are suitable for the dress. If blue or green are worn, they should be relieved with trimmings of dark furs. Silk is not suitable for skating costume. To avoid suffering from cold feet, the boot should be amply loose.

—OUR DEPORTMENT, 1882

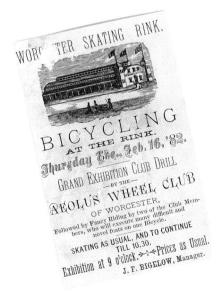

Manly consideration for womanly timidity and inferiority of strength is the first rule of good manners where men and women wheel together.

—ENCYCLOPAEDIA OF ETIQUETTE, 1901

AT THE OPERA, THEATER OR PUBLIC LECTURE

If it is a promenade concert or opera, the lady should be invited to promenade during the intermission. If she decline, the gentleman must retain his position by her side. The custom of going out alone between the acts to visit the refreshment-room cannot be too strongly reprehended. It is little less than an insult to the lady.

Ascending a Mountain

If you are walking with a woman in the country—ascending a mountain or strolling the banks of a river,—and your companion being fatigued should choose to sit upon the ground, on no account should you allow yourself to do the same, but remain rigorously standing. To do otherwise would be flagrantly indecorous and she would probably resent it as the greatest insult.

THE KISS

The most familiar and affectionate form of salutation is the kiss. It need scarcely be said this is only proper on special occasions and between special parties.

—*DECORUM.* 1879

But how shall a good wife be won? I know that men naturally shrink from the attempt to obtain companions who are their superiors; but they will find that really intelligent women, who possess the most desirable qualities, are uniformly modest and hold their charms in modest estimation. What such women admire most in men is gallantry; not the gallantry of courts and fops, but boldness, courage, devotion, decision, and refined civility. A man's bearing wins ten superior women where his boots and brains win one.

—TITCOMB'S LETTERS TO YOUNG PEOPLE, SINGLE AND MARRIED, 1858.

Why fear to answer yes?
This circling bond a charm.
Will give existing bliss.

With plighted vows each bosom warm,
Doubt not dear maid, no guile, with me.
But love unto eternity.

Betrothed

Being the special and select rules of conduct which apply to those who, having successfully declared their passion, exist in this happy yet delicate state of chaste anticipation

*O*nce a Victorian couple had reached tender agreement as to their mutual love and regard (and the gentleman had obtained parental consent following a frank account of his pecuniary resources and general prospects in life), the pair existed in the somewhat precarious state of betrothal. During this delicate time a man's "homage" was expected to continue, expressed in flowers, books, and continual tokens of affection, while a lady was likely to be stirred by the generous desire to help the man to whom she had promised lifelong fealty.

Technically, engaged couples were permitted a bit more freedom—to hold hands more freely, to tenderly finger a stray curl, to enjoy the occasional bliss of a kiss!—but accordingly were also subject to increased public scrutiny. Both were amply warned, for example, of the dangers of increased familiarity, which could all too easily result in folly, and engaged couples were firmly advised not to be too demonstrative of affection before marriage; even a protracted visit while in the betrothal state could endanger a lady's reputation.

For this and other reasons, Victorian engagements were inclined to be short. Besides, it was believed a long engagement allowed lovers to discover each other's imperfections . . . risky at best. "Alas! how slight a cause can move, dissention between hearts that love," they were told.

Not surprisingly, an engaged lady was told to eschew all flirtations and to avoid doing anything calculated to excite jealousy on the part of her fiancé. She might still have friends and acquaintances, still receive visits and calls, but must endeavor to conduct herself in a such a manner as to give no offense. As for an engaged gentleman, he was still obliged to be gallant to all ladies, of course, although never so attentive to any one as to cause his beloved unease. In effect, both waited—in chaste anticipation—feted and celebrated by family and friends, for the day when their two happy hearts would be made one.

The Decisive Question

At length the time arrives for the gentleman to make a proposal. If he is a good judge of human nature, he will have discovered long ere this whether his favors have been acceptably received or not, and yet he may not know positively how the lady will receive an offer of marriage. It becomes him, therefore, to propose. —HILL'S MANUAL. 1884

Two Valentines—"What does my true love say?"
—*HARPER'S WEEKLY*, FEBRUARY 18, 1871

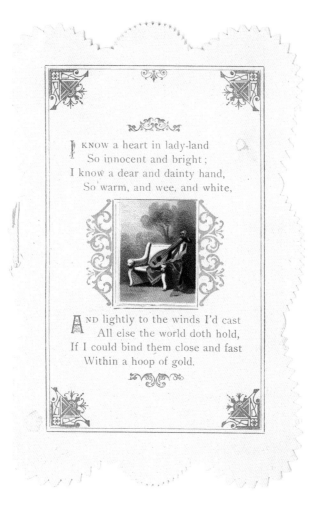

I KNOW a heart in lady-land
So innocent and bright ;
I know a dear and dainty hand,
So warm, and wee, and white,

AND lightly to the winds I'd cast
All else the world doth hold,
If I could bind them close and fast
Within a hoop of gold.

Where the acquaintance is brief, it is unwise and very presumptuous for a gentleman to make a proposal to a young lady; all such pro-posals come from mere adventurers and should be rejected; and a lady who would accept—on first sight, hardly possesses the discretion needed to make a good wife. —POLITE LIFE AND ETIQUETTE. 1891

The girl who has just entered upon a happy engagement probably feels that she is at the acme of bliss and it is quite likely that she is. Since the goal of an engagement is marriage, there is a prevalent impression that the latter state will be more joyous than the first.

—*CORRECT SOCIAL USAGE*, 1907

All the world loves a lover, and the betrothed pair, in their ensphered Eden, occupied with their roseate dreams, living in anticipation, are objects of interest to elderly people whom they perhaps do not know, but who recognize their relation by unerring and infallible tokens.

The diamond, most precious and enduring of stones, is the usual engagement ring, and its sparkling dew drop on a maiden's finger announces to her circle that her betrothal has taken place.

—WINSOME WOMANHOOD. 1900

Society becomes very uninteresting to the newly engaged couple who are never weary of one another; still they must try to behave as though some slight interest attached to the outside world.

—MANNERS AND RULES OF GOOD SOCIETY. 1913

A young man has no right to put a slight upon his future bride by appearing in public with other ladies while she remains neglected at home. He should attend no other lady when she needs his services; she should accept no other escort when he is at liberty to attend her.

—OUR DEPORTMENT. 1882

A man is what a woman makes him and if she allows him to get into bad habits during the engagement, she will never be able to cure him of them during her married life.

A man is not always at his best when he is just engaged and a girl is in a constant state of anxiety for fear that he may not please her relations. A man should take the trouble to please the friends of his fiancée, although it is difficult for him not to be so engrossed in her as to forget that other people exist in the world.

—MANNERS AND RULES OF GOOD SOCIETY. 1913

Grace: What's that piece of string on your finger for?
Ethel: Oh, that's to remember I'm engaged. Frank's gone to New York to get the ring and I don't want to forget it while he's away—

—HARPER'S BAZAR. OCTOBER 14, 1893

Demonstrations of Affection

*It may be well to hint that a lady should not be too demonstrative
of her affection during the days of engagement. There is always the
chance of a slip 'twixt the cup and the lip; and overt demonstrations
of love are not pleasant to remember by a young lady if the man to
whom they are given by any chance fails to become her husband.*

*An honorable man will never tempt his future bride to any such
demonstration. He will always maintain a respectful and decorous
demeanor toward her.*   —DECORUM. 1879

*I suppose that in every young man's mind there exists the hope and
the expectation of marriage. When a young man pretends to me that
he has no wish to marry, and that he never expects to marry, I
always infer one of two things: that he lies, and is really very anxious for marriage, or that his heart has been polluted by association
with unworthy women.*   —TITCOMB'S LETTERS, 1858

Wedded Bliss

*Being the codes and canons of behavior accorded one's
chosen, cherished companion in life's pilgrimage,
and which, when followed, will render a Home happy,
assuring both prosperity and joy*

*Ring, sweetest bells, in merry peals,
Ring for the love that the eye reveals,
Ring for the vows that make two one,
Ring for the best day under the sun.*

Thus the Victorians celebrated the all-congenial joys of the wedding day; thus they looked happily ahead to the sacred pleasures and responsibilities of married life. To the wife lay the duty and privilege of rendering the home happy; to the husband, the admonition to consider his beloved the light of his domestic circle, letting no clouds obscure the region in which she presided. Both were expected to continue the courtesies and small civilities of courtship throughout the course of wedded life, where a dignified if affectionate formality ruled.

As late as the 1890s it was considered improper for a married gentleman to refer familiarly to "my wife" except when speaking to the most intimate of acquaintances. Instead, she was accorded the proper respect of being spoken of as "Mrs." In private, a husband had the privilege of his wife's Christian name, or, it was suggested, he might address her as "my dear."

Old-fashioned considerations pervaded Victorian married life. He bowed to her—a stately, graceful bend—offered her his arm when out walking, and never permitted her the indignity of being seen carrying a package of any kind. "The husband, in fact, should act toward his wife as becomes a perfect gentleman, regarding her as "the best lady in the land" to whom, above all other earthly beings he owed paramount allegiance," he was told. To be ever kind, ever attentive, to sacrifice personal comfort for her happiness, out of true affection and devotion, was his willing duty. She, in turn, while previously admired for her engaging manners, grace on the dance floor, or skill at music, now assumed the moral role of womanhood: to inspire her life's partner with high and noble thoughts and lofty aims, to lead him to the tender enjoyment of sacred home comforts and domestic happiness.

CONSTANCY.
There is nothing but death
Our affections can sever,
And till life's latest breath
Love shall bind us for ever.

Marriage is intended to bring joy. The married life is meant to be the happiest, fullest, purest, richest life. It is God's own ideal of completeness. It was when he saw that it was not good for man to be alone that woman was made and brought to him to supply what was lacking. —HOMEMAKING, 1882

AN OFFERING OF LOVE.

ETIQUETTE BETWEEN HUSBANDS AND WIVES

Let the rebuke be preceded by a kiss.

Do not require a request to be repeated.

Never should both be angry at the same time.

Let each strive always to accommodate each other.

Bestow your warmest sympathies in each other's trials.

Make your criticism in the most loving manner possible.

Make no display of the sacrifices you make for each other.

Never make a remark calculated to bring ridicule upon the other.

Never deceive; confidence, once lost, can never be wholly regained.

Always use the most gentle and loving words when addressing each other.

Let each study what pleasures can be bestowed upon the other during the day.

Always leave home with a tender good-bye and loving words. They may be the last.

Consult and advise together in all that comes within the experience and sphere of individuality.

Never reproach the other for an error which was done with a good motive and with the best judgement at the time.

—*HILL'S MANUAL,* 1884

CERTIFICATE OF MARRIAGE.

STATE OF IOWA.

MADISON COUNTY, *September 18th 1874.*

THIS CERTIFIES, *That on the* 17th *day of* September

A. D. 1874 *at* St Charles *in said County,*

according to law, and by authority, I duly

JOINED IN MARRIAGE

Mr Wm L. Brown

AND

Miss Mary P. McClure

IN PRESENCE OF

S. M. Kennedy *and* Jas M. Lytle

Given under my hand the 18th *day of* September *A. D.* 1874.

Silas Johnson

pastor pres. Ch. Indianola

I with rapture view this pair,
Hymens joys I wish to share,
Let Cupid guide you to the spot,
To make me blest in mortal lot,
My earthly Angel, you shall be,
I'll love, but love no one but the.

Angels hover about the marriage altar and hush their songs while hands are clasped and holy vows plighted and then spread their sheltering wings over the happy pair as they start out together on the voyage of life. —HOMEMAKING, 1882

One white day in a girl's life is peculiarly sacred as her own, her pearl of days. The years of her youth have led up to this processional, joyful, filled with preparation, but all in the process of nature, fitting her for a woman's coronation. —WINSOME WOMANHOOD, 1900

The wedding day is one that should ever be remembered and held sacred among life's anniversaries. It is the day whose benediction should fall on all other days to the end of life. It should stand out in the calendar bright with all the brightness of love and gratitude. The memory of the wedding-hour in a happy married life should shine like a star, even in old age.

—*HOMEMAKING*, 1882

An Emblem this of happy life
Unknown to care, devoid of strife
Where Beauty's self reposes

May it prove so, with you and I
If Wedlock's sweets we chance to try
With love among the Roses.

As Roses other flowers excel
So Wedlock's charms still wear the bell
Among Joys of human life

No Pleasures can with those compare
Which faithful love alone can share
Twixt happy Man and Wife.

On the wedding day, the happy pair should have about them their truest friends, those whom they desire to hold in close relationships in their after life. It is no time for insincerity; it is no place for empty professions of friendship. —HILL'S MANUAL. 1884

Never should a wife display her best conduct, her accomplishments, her smiles, and her best nature, exclusively away from home.

Beware of entrusting the confidence of your household to outside parties. The moment you discuss the faults of your husband with another, that moment an element of discord has been admitted which will one day rend your family circle.

Marry a person who is your equal in social position. If there be a difference either way, let the husband be superior to the wife. It is difficult for a wife to love and honor a person whom she is compelled to look down upon. —HILL'S MANUAL. 1884

Mr. and Mrs. Simon Stroup
request your presence
at the marriage of their daughter,
Norea J.
to
Mr. Charles J. Kepner,
Tuesday evening, December 26, 1899
at eight o'clock,
Moore St., Millersburg, Pa.

Hattie 1854   1907
Golden Wedding
William & Mary Cunningham

Husband and wife should remember, when starting out upon their newly wedded life, that they are to be life companions, that the affection they have possessed and expressed as lovers must ripen into a life-long devotion to one another's welfare and happiness, that the closest friendship must be begotten from their early love, and that each must live and work for the other. —OUR DEPORTMENT, 1882

The more of a man you become, and the more of manliness you become capable of exhibiting in your association with women, the better wife you will be able to obtain; and one year's possession of a really noble specimen of her sex, is worth nine hundred and ninety-nine years of a sweet creature with two ideas in her head and nothing new to say about either of them. —TITCOMB'S LETTERS, 1858

Yet the marriage relation is put above the filial, for a man to leave his father and mother, give up his old home with all its sacred ties and memories and cleave to his wife. After marriage, a husband's first and highest duties are to his wife, and a wife's to her husband. The two are to live for each other. Life is to be lost for life.

—HOMEMAKING, 1882

As far away alone I roam,
My thoughts are filled
with love and home.
I listen in the sunset glow
For words and songs of
"long ago."
I think of all most dear to me,
And with them all come
thoughts of
thee.

Any old time is love time.

Notes

The majority of the embossed die-cut scraps and some of the valentines that appear in this work are from a single source: a cloth-covered Victorian scrapbook, patent dated March 1876. Therefore, they represent the taste and aesthetic of the individual collector who assembled it during the late 1870s and early 1880s. Material on its pages includes pieces dated 1881 and 1882, which, along with the colorations, style, and method of arrangement help to pinpoint the time of its assembly.

Front matter:
p. i—"Cupid with Cornucopia" trade card. Reverse side advertises corsets, kid gloves, $1.00 purchases, and a new carpet room. John A. Roberts, 171 Genesee St., Utica, N.Y. Verse, from a miniature hand-colored calling card, c. 1850, courtesy J. L. Cassullo.
p. ii—Verse from pop-up valentine (p. 5), unsigned, c. 1875.
p. iii—Pop-up valentine, unsigned, c. 1875.
p. vi—Heart-shaped hand-colored unfolding paper token, c. 1850.
p. viii—Pop-up valentine, c. 1875.
p. x—Trade card for Fleischmann and Co.'s Compressed Yeast; date of issue, January 1, 1897.

Introduction:
References in this Introduction from *Hill's Manual of Social and Business Forms*.
p. 3—Gilded and embossed card and embossed bookmark, c. 1875–80. Chromolithographed die-cut card ("To One I Love"), produced in Bavaria, courtesy Inez and Jack Golden collection.
p. 4—Gilded card with hand-colored bride, c. 1855.
p. 6—Miniature hand-colored calling card, c. 1850.
p. 8—Late Victorian calling card.
p. 9—Miniature hand-colored calling card, c. 1850.

Chapter One: Courtship, Manners & Morals
p. 10—Victorian cabinet card, Ella Carmen Bliss, Oak Park and Boulder, Co. (in pencil), Canova Studio. Antique lockets and trinkets, courtesy Antiques by Dorene and the British Treasure Shop.
p. 12—Die-cut miniature acquaintance card, wood engraving, c. 1860 courtesy J. L. Cassullo.
p. 14—Hand-colored aquatint, published in England (c. 1840), part of a series known as "Unrequited Love Series." Courtesy the Inez and Jack Golden collection.
p. 15—Valentine and verse, c. 1880, from the collection of Nancy Rosin.
p. 16—Postcard, "The Only Two at the Opera," Frederick A. Stokes Co., unused, c. 1909.
p. 18–19—Illustrations and verses, J. Wrigley, 25 Miller St., Manchester, c. 1845–55.

Chapter 2: Tokens of Love & Romantic Enticements

Chapter 3: Love's Proper Pastimes
All references in text, *Our Deportment*, 1882.

p. 63—"Entertainments for the Home," booklet produced by the Estey Piano Co., New York, 1885.

p. 64—Dance program for reception and ball at Mechanics' Hall, Manchester, N.H., Friday evening, February 24, 1893, courtesy J. L. Cassullo; invitation, 55th Anniversary Ball, December 14, 1871.

p. 64—Invitation to a basket picnic, June 26, 1876.

p. 65—Trade Card, H. O. Neill & Co, for ladies' hats, c. 1880.

p. 66—Admission ticket to ice rink, 1898–99 season, courtesy J. L. Cassullo; bicycling invitation, February 16, 1882.

p. 67—Bookmark, c. 1875, courtesy J. L. Cassullo.

p. 68—Gilded trade card, Nathan Ford Pianos and Organs, St. Paul, Minn., 1875–85.

p. 68—Trade card, Estey Organ Co., c. 1885.

Chapter Four: Betrothed
All references in text, *Hills Manual*, 1884

p. 69—Hand-colored aquatint, published in England (c. 1840), part of a series known as "Unrequited Love Series." Courtesy the Inez and Jack Golden collection.

p. 70—Unidentified Victorian cabinet card, C. S. Obst Studio, Pittsfield, Ill. Antique trinkets, Antiques by Dorene and the British Treasure Shop.

p. 72—Hand-colored miniature calling card, c. 1850.

p. 73—Embossed and gilded postcards, top, postmarked February 7, 1910; bottom, February 14, 1910, both courtesy J. L. Cassullo.

p. 74—Valentine, c. 1880.

p. 75—Valentine, collection of Nancy Rosin.

p. 79—Valentine, c. 1880, collection of Nancy Rosin.

Chapter Five: Wedded Bliss
References in text, *Winsome Womanhood*, 1900; *Hills Manual*, 1884.

p. 80—Victorian cabinet card, Gregory Wick, Leading Photographer, 217 Broad St., Norwich, N.Y.

p. 87—Lithographed card, c. 1890, courtesy J. L. Cassullo.

p. 83—Embossed and gilded cards, c. 1875, courtesy J. L. Cassullo.

p. 85—Trade Card, c. 1890.

p. 86—Certificate of Marriage, September, 1874.

p. 87—Hand-colored aquatint, c. 1840.

p. 88—Trade card for Merrick Thread Co., depicting President Grover Cleveland and White House bride Frances Folsom Cleveland, c. 1886.

p. 89—Valentine, c. 1880–90.

p. 90–91—Hand-colored engravings, c. 1840. Courtesy the Inez and Jack Golden collection.

p. 93—Wedding invitation, December 26, 1899; calling card, c. 1875; Small card to Ruth from Edna and Lillian, c. 1880; Golden Wedding Anniversary, 1854–1907, courtesy J. L. Cassullo.

p. 95—Marriage certificate, December 14, 1858; wedding card, 1880.

p. 96–97—Valentine, c. 1885.

p. 98—"Any old time is love time," postcard, postmarked June 28, 1911, from Edith to Clarence Helin.

Bibliography

BENHAM, GEORGENE CORRY. *Polite Life & Etiquette or What Is Right and the Social Arts.* Chicago and Philadelphia: Louis Benham & Co., 1891.

Correct Social Usage, A Course of Instruction in Good Form, Style and Deportment, by eighteen distinguished authors. New York: The New York Society of Self Culture. Vol. 1, 1905; Vol. 2, 1907. Originally published 1903.

Decorum, A Practical Treatise on Etiquette & Dress of the Best American Society. New York, Chicago and Cincinnati: J. A. Ruth & Co., 1879. First edition, 1877. Sold only by subscription.

GOW, ALEX M. *Good Morals and Gentle Manners.* Cincinnati and New York: Van Antwerp, Bragg & Co., 1873.

HARLAND, MARION, AND VIRGINIA VAN DE WATER. *Everyday Etiquette, a Practical Manual of Social Usages.* Indianapolis: The Bobbs-Merrill Co., 1905.

HARLAND, MARION. *Eve's Daughters, or Common Sense for Maid, Wife, and Mother.* New York: John R. Anderson & Henry S. Allen Publishers, No. 55 Chambers Street, 1882.

Hill's Manual of Social and Business Forms. Chicago: 1884. Originally published in 1874.

HOLT, EMILY. *Encyclopedia of Etiquette, A Book of Manners for Everyday Use.* Garden City, New York: Doubleday, Page & Co., 1901-15.

Manners & Rules of Good Society, A Compendium of the Proper Etiquette to be Observed on Every Occasion (no author). New York: The New York Book Company, 1913.

MILLER, D.D., THE REV. J. R. *Home-making.* Presbyterian Board of Publication, No. 1334. Chestnut St., Philadelphia, Pa., 1882.

The People's Valentine Writer, by a Literary Lady. New York: T. W. Strong, 98 Nassau Street. Boston: G. W. Cottrel & Co., c. 1860.

SANGSTER, MARGARET E. *Winsome Womanhood.* New York, Chicago, Toronto: Fleming H. Revell Company, 1900.

TITCOMB, ESQUIRE, TIMOTHY. *Titcomb's Letters to Young People, Single and Married.* New York: Charles Scribner, No. 124 Grand St., 1858.

True Politeness, The Ladies' Book of Etiquette. No author. London: Darton and Clark, Holborn Hill. Philadelphia: George S. Appleton, 148 Chestnut Street. Probably 1878.

YOUNG, A. M., AND JOHN R. YOUNG. *Our Deportment or the Manners, Conduct & Dress of the Most Refined Society.* Compiled from the latest, reliable authorities. Revised, Enlarged & Illustrated. Springfield, Mass.: W. C. King & Co., Publishers, c. 1882. Originally published 1879, 1881. Note: This work, in essence, is a slightly altered version of *Decorum,* c. 1877.